Anne Frank

History Maker Bios

Laura Hamilton Waxman

LERNER PUBLICATIONS COMPANY • MINNEAPOLIS

For my Baba, Grace Levitt

Illustrations by Tad Butler

Text copyright © 2009 by Laura Hamilton Waxman

Illustrations copyright © 2009 by Lerner Publishing Group, Inc.

Lerner Publications Company
A division of Lerner Publishing Group, Inc.
241 First Avenue North
Minneapolis, MN 55401 U.S.A.

Website address: www.lernerbooks.com

Library of Congress Cataloging-in-Publication Data

Waxman, Laura Hamilton.
    Anne Frank / by Laura Hamilton Waxman.
      p.   cm. — (History maker biographies)
    Includes bibliographical references and index.
    ISBN 978–0–7613–4221–2 (lib. bdg. : alk. paper)
    1. Frank, Anne, 1929–1945. 2. Jews—Netherlands—Amsterdam—Biography—
Juvenile literature. 3. Jewish children in the Holocaust—Netherlands—
Amsterdam—Biography—Juvenile literature. 4. Holocaust, Jewish
(1939–1945)—Netherlands—Amsterdam—Juvenile literature. 5. Amsterdam
(Netherlands)—Biography—Juvenile literature. I. Title.
DS135.N6F7386 2009
940.53'18092—dc22 [B]   2008043847

Manufactured in the United States of America
1 2 3 4 5 6 – PA – 14 13 12 11 10 09

TABLE OF CONTENTS

INTRODUCTION

Anne Frank was a lively young girl living in Germany in 1933. That year, Adolf Hitler became the country's leader. Hitler felt a deep hatred for the Jewish people. Eventually he made plans to kill the Jews of Europe. This plan led to a terrible time known as the Holocaust.

Anne and her family were Jewish. They feared what Hitler and his Nazi government might do. The Franks fled to a neighboring country. But Hitler took over that country too. Anne's family went into hiding. It was a difficult time for Anne. She found comfort by writing in her diary.

The Nazis discovered the Franks in 1944. They took Anne and her family away. Anne did not survive. But her diary did. Her powerful words remind us of her strength and courage.

This is her story.

1 A LIVELY GIRL

Anne Frank was born in Frankfurt, Germany, on June 12, 1929. Otto and Edith Frank adored their new baby girl. Anne kept her parents up at night with her crying. But she also charmed them with her bright smile.

Anne's sister, Margot, was three years older. As Anne grew, the two sisters became playmates. But Anne and Margot were very different from each other.

Margot had always been a shy, quiet, serious girl. Anne liked to be the center of attention. Her playful and spunky personality drew people to her. Unlike Margot, Anne didn't like to sit still. She needed to move around and do things. She also had strong emotions. She laughed and cried easily.

Edith Frank holds baby Anne in June 1929. Margot stands next to her mother.

In the 1920s Frankfurt was one of Germany's largest cities. It had many historical buildings.

Anne's family lived in a quiet, friendly neighborhood in Frankfurt. The Franks got along well with their neighbors. Most were Christian. Otto and Edith raised their girls to be proud of their Jewish traditions. Edith went to a Jewish synagogue each week. Yet the Franks were not a strongly religious family.

Edith Frank stayed at home to care for her daughters. Otto Frank worked hard as a businessman. Even so, he always made time for his daughters. He read to his girls and made up funny stories. He told them jokes and played games with them. He always knew how to calm Anne when she was upset.

LIEUTENANT OTTO FRANK

Many Jews in Germany loved their home country. Anne's father was one of them. He had fought in the German army during World War I (1914–1918). This war took place in Europe. Otto bravely led other German soldiers to fight for their homeland. But Germany lost the war. After that, the country went through some hard times. Many Germans longed for the country to be strong and powerful once again.

Anne had a good life in Germany. But the country wasn't doing very well by 1933. There weren't enough jobs for everyone. Without jobs, people couldn't afford to buy the things they needed. Businesses shut down. Even more people lost their jobs. And prices for food and clothing went up and up.

The Franks worried about the country's problems. So did other Germans. Some of them were very angry. They blamed the Jews for all the troubles. One of those people was Adolf Hitler.

As Germany's new leader, Hitler inspired large crowds with his thundering speeches. He said that he would make Germany stronger than ever. He promised more jobs and a better way of life. He promised to make Germany a world power once again. His deep hatred for the Jews included other groups of people too. He disliked anyone whom he did not think was a pure German. He wanted to rid Germany of these people.

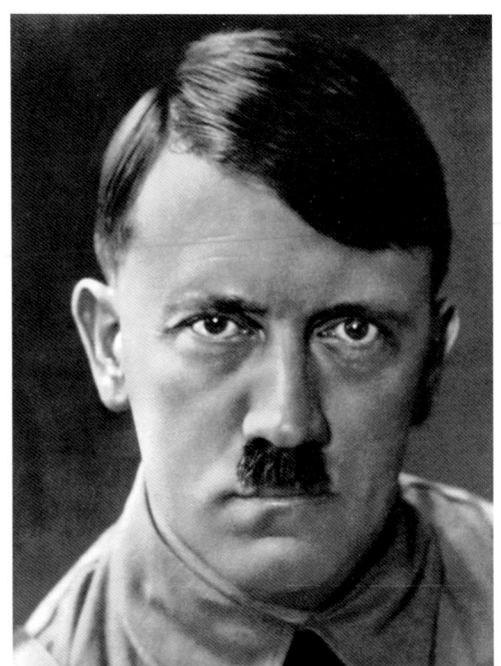

Adolf Hitler was born in Austria. He moved to Germany when he was twenty-four years old.

German soldiers put up a poster telling Germans not to buy things from a store owned by Jewish people.

Hitler scared the Franks. His new government became known as the Nazi government. The Nazis began to separate Jewish people from other Germans. They fired all Jewish workers from jobs in the government, schools, and universities. In classrooms, Jewish students had to sit in a corner by themselves. Hitler planned to force Jewish children out of school altogether.

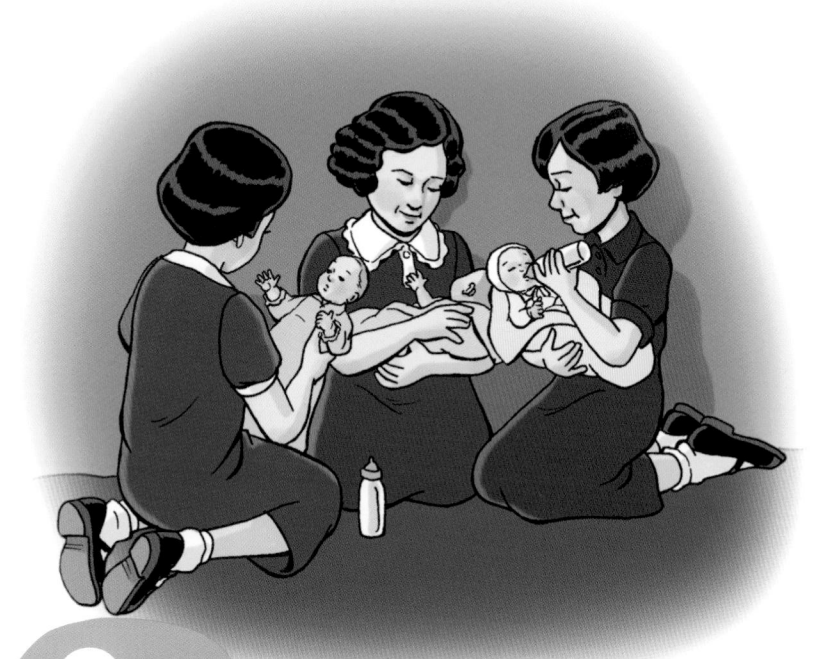

2 ESCAPE FROM GERMANY

The Franks moved to the Netherlands later in 1933. Jewish people had always been treated well in this European country. The Franks hoped they would be out of danger there.

Anne's family moved to this neighborhood in Amsterdam. Anne walked in this square almost every day.

Anne's parents found an apartment in the large city of Amsterdam. Otto started a new business. He and his family slowly settled into their new life. They learned the Dutch language. They began to make new friends.

Many other Jewish families also fled from Germany to Amsterdam. Most of them settled in the same neighborhood as Anne's family. The Franks became a part of this growing Jewish community.

Anne turned five during the summer of 1934. She started school that fall. She was not as good a student as Margot. But she had a lot of fun. She quickly got to know her classmates. She drew them in with her lively chatter and laughter. It didn't matter who was Jewish and who wasn't. Anne had all kinds of friends.

Anne's two best friends were Hannah and Susanne. They spent many hours together. People jokingly called them Anne, Hanne, and Sanne. They played games such as hopscotch, tag, and catch. They rode bikes and roller skates. They bought one another treats at the local ice cream parlor.

Anne loved her school. In this class picture, she sits in the back, just in front of her teacher.

Life was good for Anne and other Jews in Amsterdam. But the Jews in Germany were suffering terribly. Many Germans had become followers of Hitler's Nazi government. They marched through the streets and shouted hateful words against the Jews. Sometimes they beat up Jewish citizens or even killed them. They smashed and burned synagogues. They destroyed Jewish businesses. Jewish families feared for their lives.

Followers of the Nazi government smashed the windows at this Jewish business in 1938.

Anne and her family heard about what was happening in Germany from news reports on the radio. In 1938, they learned that Hitler's power had spread. That year he took over the neighboring country of Austria. After that, he took over another country and another. It seemed that he wanted to take control of all of Europe. In September 1939, the leaders of France and Great Britain declared war on Germany. This war became known as World War II (1939–1945).

WAR OF THE WORLD

Great Britain and France were the first to fight against Germany in World War II. But many countries took part. The former Soviet Union (a union of fifteen republics, including Russia), the United States, and China sided with Great Britain and France. Japan and Italy sided with Germany. Other smaller countries also fought in the war. The fighting lasted for nearly six years.

Trucks full of Nazi soldiers drive through Amsterdam in May 1940.

Hitler refused to let anyone stop him. His Nazi government continued to take over other countries. On May 10, 1940, the Nazis invaded the Netherlands as well. Anne's parents were very frightened. They had left Germany to escape the Nazis. Once again they were under Hitler's power.

At first, very little changed for the Franks and other Jews. Anne and Margot kept going to school. They still played with their friends. They led their normal lives.

The changes came slowly. The Nazis began to make new laws in the Netherlands. One law said that Jews could no longer go to movie theaters. This upset Anne terribly. She had always loved movies and movie stars. She had a big photo collection of Hollywood actresses and other famous people.

Deanna Durbin (CENTER) was one of Anne's favorite movie stars. Anne hung this picture from the movie FIRST LOVE on her wall.

The Nazis also made it a crime for Jews to go to public places. They weren't allowed at parks, beaches, or swimming pools. They couldn't even ride in cars, on streetcars, or on bicycles. Anne and her family had to give up many activities they loved.

Another new rule said that Jewish and non-Jewish students had to go to separate schools. Anne was twelve years old. She had to leave behind her old school. She had to say good-bye to many of her non-Jewish classmates. She soon lost touch with them.

The Nazis forced Jews to live and do business only on certain streets in Amsterdam.

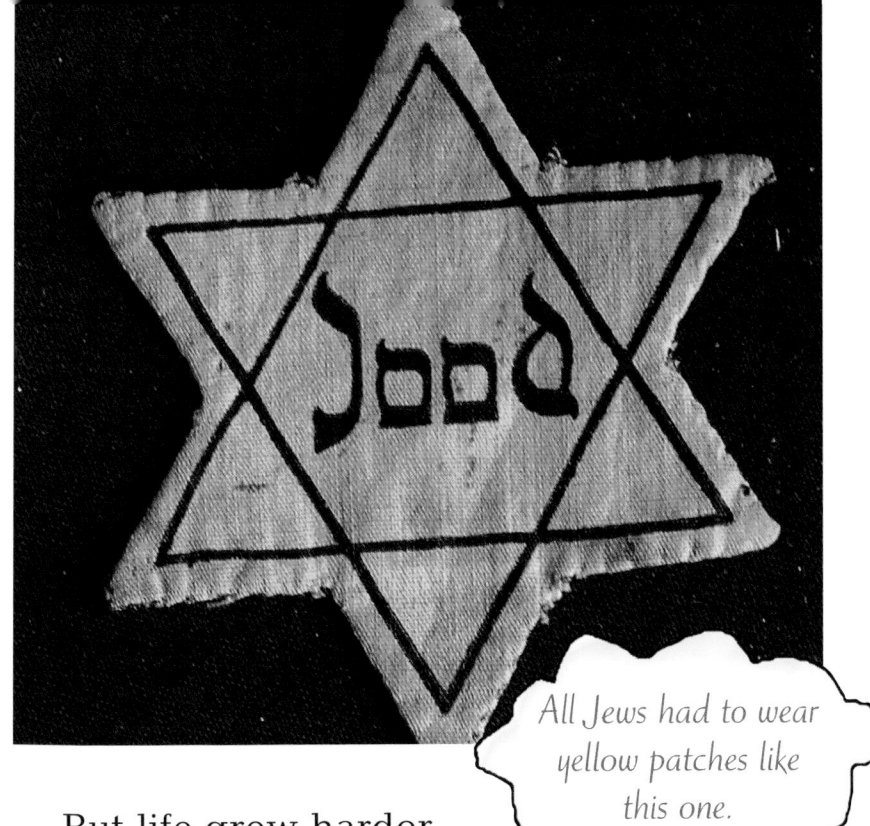

All Jews had to wear yellow patches like this one.

But life grew harder still. In April 1942, the Nazis created another rule. All Jewish people had to wear a yellow patch on their clothing. On the patch was the Dutch word for Jew.

The patch was shaped like the Star of David. This star is a symbol of the Jewish religion. But the Nazis used the star to shame the Jews. They wanted to make the Jewish people feel like outsiders. Anne and her family feared what the Nazis would do next.

3 WAR CHANGES EVERYTHING

Anne turned thirteen years old on June 12, 1942. Her parents gave her a wonderful birthday celebration. They didn't want the Nazis to ruin their daughter's special day. Anne received many presents from her family and friends. Her favorite gift was a brand-new diary.

Anne began writing in her diary right away. She had a gift for using language. She enjoyed putting her thoughts into words.

Anne wrote about her classmates and friends. She wrote about the boy she had a crush on. And she wrote about life for the Jews under Nazi control.

Like other Jews, Anne had gotten used to the Nazis' rules. She didn't like them. But she had learned to live with them. She didn't know that a new danger was coming.

This is a picture of Anne's diary. It has a red plaid cover.

The Nazis had begun sending Jewish people to terrible places called concentration camps. The prisoners in these camps were horribly mistreated. They were given very little food. They lived in crowded, dirty buildings. And they were forced to work long hours. Worst of all, many prisoners were put to death. Hitler was carrying out his plan to kill the Jews of Europe.

A Jewish family leaves for a Nazi concentration camp in the early 1940s. Nazi soldiers allowed them to take only a few belongings with them.

Otto Frank ran his business in this building. He sold herbs and other cooking products.

Anne's parents did not yet know about Hitler's plan. But they guessed that the camps were bad places. They had already made their own secret plan. They had begun setting up a hiding place for the family. That way, they could escape from the Nazis if they needed to.

The hiding place was in some back rooms of Otto Frank's business. This part of the building became known as the Secret Annex. No one could see the annex from the street. So it was a good place to hide.

Little by little, the Franks snuck in some of their furniture. They also brought in things such as books, dishes, and canned food.

On July 5, 1942, the family received very bad news. The Nazis had ordered Margot to go to a concentration camp. Margot was only sixteen years old. Her parents were determined to protect her.

The Franks got up early the next morning. Margot biked to the hiding place with a family friend. Anne walked there with her parents.

The Franks couldn't carry their clothing in suitcases. Nazi soldiers patrolled the streets. They would notice a Jewish family with luggage. Instead, the Franks had to wear all the clothing they needed. Anne wrote, "I was wearing two undershirts, three pairs of underpants, a dress, a skirt, a jacket, a raincoat, two pairs of stockings, heavy shoes, a cap, a scarf and lots more." She also brought her diary.

THE HOLOCAUST

Hitler's Nazis set up concentration camps all over Europe. The worst ones were in Germany and German-controlled Poland. Millions of Jews were sent to these camps. But the Nazis targeted other people too. Most concentration camp prisoners were put to death. Others died of illness or starvation. This terrible time became known as the Holocaust. About eleven million people died during the Holocaust. Six million of them were Jews. About one million of those Jews were children.

Finally, they came to Otto's workplace on 263 Prinsengracht Street. Quietly, they went upstairs to his office. Then they snuck up to the Secret Annex. It was small and stuffy. But they would have to get used to it. They didn't know how long they would need to hide.

4 THE SECRET ANNEX

Anne's life had changed overnight. She could no longer see her friends or neighbors. She couldn't run or play outside. She couldn't feel the wind or the rain or the sun. She had lost her freedom. But she hadn't lost her spunk. Anne had as much energy as ever. She used it to make the best of things.

Earlier, Otto had snuck in some of Anne's favorite pictures. She decided to put these photographs on the wall of her bedroom. Anne also helped her family organize the Secret Annex. She moved furniture and unpacked boxes. She helped scrub the floors and roll out carpets.

This is Anne's bedroom. She decorated the walls with her favorite pictures.

This model shows the second floor of the Secret Annex. Anne shared this floor with her family and Fritz Pfeffer.

The Franks were lucky. They had a place to hide from the Nazis. Many Jews were still in danger. Anne's parents agreed to squeeze in four more people. One of them was a man named Hermann Van Pels. He worked with Anne's father. Hermann came with his wife, Auguste, and his son, Peter. The fourth person was a Jewish dentist named Fritz Pfeffer.

These eight people had to follow strict rules. Otherwise, the workers in the building might discover them. The Nazis had begun rewarding people who helped them find Jews in hiding. A worker might find out about the annex and turn in everyone.

The eight people hiding in the Secret Annex shared this single toilet.

Everyone in the annex had to wake by seven o'clock. They each took a turn using the bathroom and getting dressed. Then they ate breakfast together. But they had to hurry. The workers arrived at eight thirty. After that, Anne and the others had to stay as still and quiet as possible. They couldn't even flush the toilet. They didn't want to risk anyone hearing them.

Anne filled those quiet hours by studying and reading. She, Margot, and Peter learned English and French. They also worked on math, geography, and history.

All that sitting still and being quiet was hard for Anne. Each morning, she longed for the workers' lunch break to come. Then the men in the warehouse left the building. For an hour and a half, the people in the annex could talk, stretch, and use the bathroom.

At two o'clock, the workers returned. Anne and the others had to be silent once again. At night, the workers went home. Anne could finally relax. But she couldn't go outside and breathe the fresh air. She couldn't take a long walk or ride her bicycle. She couldn't even look out the annex's few dirty windows. No one outside could ever see them.

Anne spent many hours reading here in the crowded kitchen and dining area of the annex.

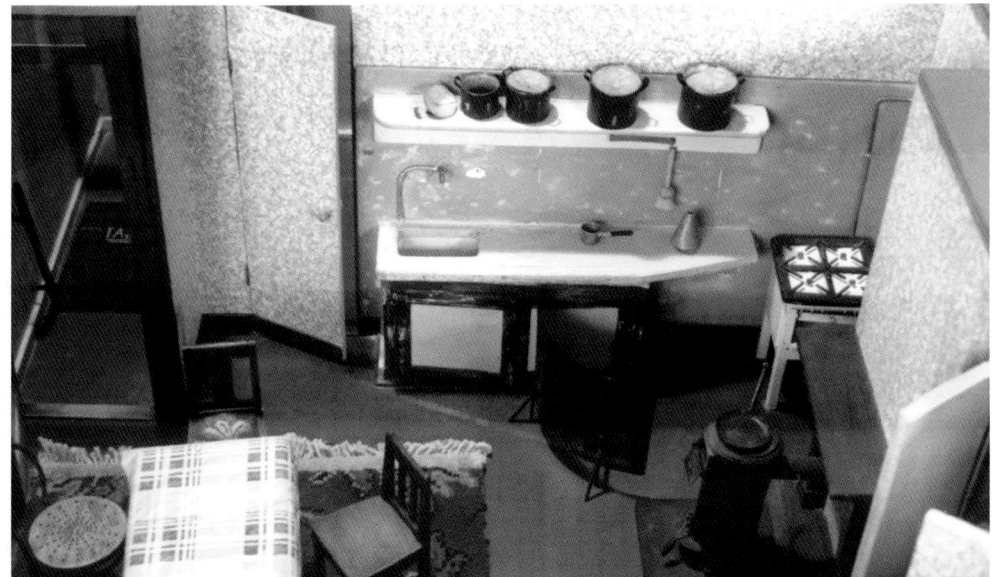

Otto Frank (CENTER) sits with (LEFT TO RIGHT) Miep Gies, Johannes Kleiman, Victor Kugler, and Bep Voskuijl

Only Otto's most trusted employees knew about the Secret Annex. They were Miep Gies, Victor Kugler, Johannes Kleiman, and Bep Voskuijl. These brave people risked terrible punishment for helping Jews. They snuck in food, milk, clothing, books, and magazines. Best of all, they visited with Anne and the others in the Secret Annex.

During these visits, Anne became a chatterbox. She asked the visitors question after question. Did they know what had happened to her cat? Were people asking about her? What was the latest news on the war? What was happening to her friends?

Anne missed spending time with people her own age. She often felt lonely. She decided to write letters to an imaginary friend. She called this friend Kitty.

Anne poured her heart out to Kitty. She described her life in the Secret Annex. She wrote about her fears. She wrote about her hopes and dreams. "When I write I can shake off all my cares," she told Kitty. "My sorrows disappear."

Anne also kept pictures and letters in her diary.

Anne wanted to grow up and fall in love. She wanted to travel and see the world. She also wanted to become a successful author. "I want to be useful or bring enjoyment to all people," she wrote, "even to those I've never met." She decided her first book would be called "The Secret Annex." She thought people might want to read about her life in hiding.

The hidden door to the Secret Annex kept the Franks safe.

Time passed slowly inside the Secret Annex. A year went by. Another began. Anne turned fourteen and then fifteen. It became harder and harder to stay cooped up all day and night. It was also hard never to have any space to herself. Anne wrote: "I'm longing—really longing—for everything: conversation, freedom, friends, being alone."

Anne's biggest hope was that the war would end soon. She and the others listened to news reports on the radio. In the summer of 1944, they heard some good news. Germany was in danger of losing the war. If Germany lost, the Netherlands would be free again. Then they could come out of hiding.

This news thrilled Anne. "Now at last things are going well!" she wrote excitedly. Perhaps the war was finally coming to an end.

5 A Diary Left Behind

On August 4, 1944, Anne woke up as usual. She took her turn in the bathroom and had a small breakfast. Then she and the others started their daily routine of silence. Suddenly, they heard a noise at the door. The door burst open. In rushed the Nazi police. The Nazis had discovered the little group of Jews hiding in the Secret Annex.

The police arrested them all. Anne and the others had to leave right away. They had time to take only a few belongings. Anne left her diary behind.

The Nazis sent Anne and her family to a prison camp in the Netherlands. Anne was very scared. But she couldn't help being a little happy too. At last, she could stare up at the sky. She could see the trees and feel the rain. She also enjoyed being around other people. Thousands of Jews were imprisoned in the same camp.

Hundreds of Jews line up after arriving at the Westerbork prison camp. The Franks were sent there in 1944.

A month later, the Nazis stuffed the Franks onto a crowded train. The train took a thousand Jews to a German concentration camp in Poland. This camp was called Auschwitz. In Auschwitz, the Nazis put most prisoners to death.

Anne and her family had to give up all their belongings. They were given thin prison uniforms. Their heads were shaved. Worst of all, the Nazis separated men from women. Anne couldn't see her father anymore.

At the Auschwitz camp, electrified fences surrounded the crowded buildings where prisoners were kept.

The Bergen-Belsen camp was so crowded that many prisoners, including Anne and Margot, lived in tents.

Weeks later, the Nazis separated Anne and Margot from their mother too. The sisters were sent to a camp called Bergen-Belsen. Prisoners here were not put to death. But life was very harsh. Winter was coming. Many prisoners were already sick. Disease spread quickly.

Anne and Margot had to live outside in a ratty tent. Their clothing wasn't warm enough. They didn't have nearly enough food. And they missed their parents terribly. The sisters grew very thin and ill. They both died in March 1945.

Auschwitz prisoners welcome soldiers from the Soviet Union as they enter the camp. The soldiers came to rescue them.

Germany lost the war in May 1945. Soldiers from Great Britain, Canada, France, the United States, and the Soviet Union rescued the prisoners in the concentration camps. The Holocaust came to an end.

Otto Frank was one of the rescued prisoners. Sadly, no other members of the Secret Annex had survived. Otto returned to the Netherlands. His employee and friend Miep had saved Anne's diary. She gave it to him. Anne's father was moved by what his daughter had written. He wanted the world to read her diary too.

In 1947, Anne's father published some of the diary in the Netherlands. Five years later, the book came out in the United States. It was called *Anne Frank: The Diary of a Young Girl*. The diary was soon made into a play and then a movie.

People around the world learned about Anne's story. They read her powerful words. These words gave a voice to the men, women, and children of the Holocaust.

Anne Frank died much too young. But she lives on in her writings. Her diary has inspired millions of readers through words of strength, courage, and hope.

THE ANNE FRANK HOUSE

In 1960, Anne's father helped open the Anne Frank House. This museum is inside the Secret Annex on 263 Prinsengracht Street. Visitors can see where Anne lived for two years. Some of her photo collection and diary are on display too. The museum also tells the stories of the eight people who hid in the Secret Annex.

TIMELINE

In the year...

1933 Adolf Hitler came to power in Germany in January.
The Franks decided to leave Germany.

1934 Anne started school in the Netherlands. `Age 5`

1939 World War II began.

1942 the Nazis began forcing Jews in the Netherlands to go to concentration camps.
Anne got a diary for her thirteenth birthday. `Age 13`
Margot was ordered to go to a concentration camp.
The Franks go into hiding on July 6.

1944 the people living in the Secret Annex were arrested and sent to Auschwitz.
Anne and Margot were sent to Bergen-Belsen on October 28. `Age 15`

1945 Edith died of illness at Auschwitz.
Anne and Margot died of illness in March.
Miep Gies gave Anne's diary to Otto.
World War II officially ended in September.

1947 Anne's diary was printed in Dutch.

1952 *Anne Frank: Diary of a Young Girl* was published in English in the United States.

1955 *The Diary of Anne Frank* was performed as a play.

1959 *The Diary of Anne Frank* was made into a movie.

1960 the Anne Frank House opened.

1980 Otto Frank died.

2001 the movie *Anne Frank* was aired on TV.

ANNE'S LAST WORDS

Anne spent many hours writing letters to her imaginary friend, Kitty. She wrote in Dutch, the language she spoke. Below is a photograph of her last letter in her diary. It was written on August 1, 1944. Three days later, the Nazis arrested Anne and her family. But Anne's death did not silence her. She lives on in her words.

FURTHER READING

Adams, Simon. *World War II*. New York: DK Books, 2007. This book explores the history of World War II through lively text and photographs.

Adler, David A. *We Remember the Holocaust*. New York: Henry Holt, 1995. This book is an introduction to the Holocaust told by the people who survived it.

Lehman-Wilzig, Tami. *Keeping the Promise: A Torah's Journey*. Minneapolis: Kar-Ben, 2003. The author describes the journey of a small Torah scroll as it travels from a Dutch rabbi to a Bar Mitzvah boy during the Holocaust and finally to Ilan Ramon, the first Israeli astronaut.

Lowry, Lois. *Number the Stars*. Boston: Houghton Mifflin Co., 1989. This award-winning book tells the fictional story of a Danish girl who risks her life to save her Jewish friend during the Holocaust.

Schroeder, Peter, and Dagmar Schroeder. *Six Million Paper Clips: The Making of a Children's Holocaust Memorial*. Minneapolis: Kar-Ben, 2005. This is the true story of a class of children in Tennessee who collected six million paper clips in honor of all the Jews who died during the Holocaust.

Willoughby, Susan. *The Holocaust*. Chicago: Heinemann Library, 2001. This book delves into the Holocaust and the historical events surrounding it.

WEBSITES

The Anne Frank House
http://www.annefrank.org
The museum's official website includes photos and information about Anne, the Secret Annex, and the Holocaust.

Children of the Holocaust
http://www.museumoftolerance.com/site/
pp.asp?c=arLPK7PILqF&b=249685
Part of the Museum of Tolerance, this Web page links to stories of children who lived through the Holocaust.

World War II
http://www.kidskonnect.com/content/view/288/27/
This kid-friendly website links to information about World War II.

SELECTED BIBLIOGRAPHY

Enzer, Hyman Aaron, and Sandra Solotaroff-Enzer, eds. *Anne Frank: Reflections on Her Life and Legacy.* Urbana: University of Illinois Press, 2000.

Frank, Anne. *The Diary of a Young Girl: The Definitive Edition.* New York: Doubleday, 1995.

Giep, Miep, and Alison Leslie Gold. *Anne Frank Remembered: The Story of the Woman Who Helped to Hide the Frank Family.* New York: Simon and Schuster, 1987.

Lee, Carol. *The Hidden Life of Otto Frank.* New York: William Morrow, 2003.

Lindwer, Willy. *The Last Seven Months of Anne Frank.* Translated from Dutch by Alison Meersschaert. New York: Random House, 1991.

Müller, Melissa. *Anne Frank: The Biography.* Translated by Rita Kimber and Robert Kimber. New York: Henry Holt, 1998.

INDEX

Acknowledgments

For photographs: © Anne Frank Fonds - Basel/Anne Frank House/Premium Archive/Getty Images, pp. 4, 7; © Three Lions/Hulton Archive/Getty Images, pp. 8, 18; The Illustrated London News, p. 10; © Hulton Archive/Getty Images, pp. 11, 16; Amsterdam City Archives, pp. 14, 15; Everett Collection, p. 19; © Keystone/Hulton Archive/Getty Images, p. 20; © L.E. Baskow/ZUMA Press, p. 21; © Anne Frank Fonds-Basel/Anne Frank House-Amsterdam/Getty Images, pp. 23, 26, 34; © Bettmann/CORBIS, p. 24; CSU Archives/Everett Collection, p. 25; © Topham/The Image Works, p. 30; AP Photo/Handout, Casa Anna Frank, p. 31; © The Image Works, p. 32; © Photo12/The Image Works, p. 33; Miguel Benitez/Rex Features USA, p. 35; The Granger Collection, New York, p. 36; © United States Holocaust Memorial Museum, p. 39; © KPA/ZUMA Press, p. 40; © National Archives and Records Administration, College Park, Md., p. 41; © Girella/Lapresse/ZUMA Press, p. 42; Rue des Archives/The Granger Collection, New York, p. 45.

Cover: © Anne Frank Fonds - Basel/Anne Frank House/Premium Archive/Getty Images.

For quoted material: p. 27, 35, 36, 37 (both), 45 (all), *Anne Frank, The Diary of a Young Girl: The Definitive Edition* (New York: Doubleday, 1995).